RON HAVIV
ESSAYS BY ILANA OZERNOY
AFGHANISTAN : THE ROAD TO KABUL

FOREWORD

BY ALISON MORLEY

CHAIRPERSON OF THE DOCUMENTARY PHOTOGRAPHY AND PHOTOJOURNALISM PROGRAM. THE INTERNATIONAL CENTER OF PHOTOGRAPHY. NEW YORK 2002.

Haviv's photographic synthesism is his content, his witness, his document, his intuitive and sensitive nature. He gives us clarity by allowing us to make our own journey through his framework, creating an innate sense of narrative. The photographs persuade you to persist. Captionless, one looses oneself to a different culture yet still identifies with the small universal acts – a game, a smoke, a balloon, a soccer field, a stopped clock.

Fade to the surreal, the shadow lurking over documents scattered in an abandoned al queda house; feet following a tiny concrete path that signlessly signals protection in the midst of a mine field; a blue dot lost in a brown moonscape.

His photographs demand book form. There is a deliberate sequence, each picture building upon another, creating a path for the viewer to a self altering knowledge. There are many signs but it is the wholeness that leaves a viewer ruminating on the fresh hell he has unfolded - forever shuffling this other world in one's head.

There is a sequence of pictures in his take of a Northern Alliance commander dying in a trench that is especially tough to pass over. Haviv had photographed this man moments before, standing above ground, ordering soldiers about, inches away from him. Now, a few frames later, the commander, collapsed like a rag doll, staring at the photographer, as his camera stares back, the last person he will probably ever see. The shock, the disappointment, the utter simplicity of dying now gazing up at us from the page, only months later.

It is an exceptional photograph, not because the man is dying - we know all war photojournalists have witnessed this before - it is exceptional because Haviv always strives for invisibility. Rarely do people in his photographs acknowledge this act of picture taking. It is a difficult accomplishment in my mind. Though when asked, Haviv always says that there is so much going on, from shelling to anger to grief that people are oblivious to him.

But where Ron Haviv stands seems impossible to ignore. There is a forced intimacy with the abstract, like a painting that starts to take on recognizable shapes after you stare at it a while. The thing most foreign becoming the familiar; where the melding of heart and mind pinch together to humanize that what seems impossible to grasp.

The craziness unfolds further, people standing on the top of their haphazard forts instead of hiding behind them as childhood memory helps me recall is the sensible stance. Each side conversing on walkie talkies, like neighbors and friends they have always known. Until something blows. The confusion escalates as you begin to see the ancient landscape that decades of turmoil have rolled back in time and slowly made these people seemingly apathetic to death.

Haviv is aware of anything that is contrived for the camera. He is a purist - he shoots it as he breathes it. His only goal being for

Vital Signs

This digital age is a perplexing time, especially for the photojournalist. So many aspects of a picture could be altered, it is often difficult to trust what stands as evidence. What makes Ron Haviv an honest journalist, what distinguishes him, is his dedication to making a historical and accurate document; just as a writer does with the words he chooses to draw from. It is up to these individuals to weigh the balance of how something could be perceived as one thing and the reality – another thing entirely. Journalists help shape our image of the world. Each visual decision a photographer makes matters; what he allows in or pushes out of a frame can be a revealing fragment of history. We are a civilization marked by these decisions.

the world to look after in judgment. Upon examining his photographs, one must remember that nothing is arranged; he does not direct. The child that holds the ball. The soldier that is firing. The Koran that stands open in the middle of nowhere. The imperative context of these images fuel the trust we assume with Haviv.

There is no intentional shock value woven into these images, just the light and the truth as Haviv saw it that day. The color can be lush, the people handsome and strong - it is, after all, the world we all still share. Trying to understand these photographs is the only way I know how we can evolve, how we can love, how we can move forward.

In "Afghanistan:The Road To Kabul" we find the bizarre Afghanistan that hid its women and allowed the destruction of its own art by the Taliban, as if to rewrite history, to reorder life as we know it. What was left to shock? What was left to make us look? Much like a child destroying her

favorite doll to get her mother's attention; something hurts and we are not listening. Well, now we are. It hit home finally and has drawn the attention of people who previously might not have cared to examine a land and people such that Afghanistan gives us.

Just as eyes were shutting to photojournalism, they have now been pried open by the most unimaginable action that millions of people witnessed, together. Thousands of ordinary people became reporters of history on September 11th and my hope is that they will indeed never forget.

For it seems impossible to me to ignore the power that photojournalism stands fast to inform the world. The lasting memory of a single image will always resonate long after the television news videos have faded. The resilient and unyielding efforts that make Haviv persist in this quest to bring compassion and understanding to a daily world that can be brutal, unspeakable and unimaginable. Haviv's sharply observed images give us the opportunity to rethink, to question, not to necessarily answer.

There is a part of me that insists we will look longer now - as a teacher, a believer in the power of photography and a student of man's inhumanity to man, that we hold these images as graven heartaches of our time on this earth, that we must look at these broken parts and make others continue to look, less history eagerly repeats itself.

INTRODUCTION
BY ILANA OZERNOY

It begins with
the jolt of an old,
metal barge,
as it slams into the
Afghan side
of the riverbank.
A single shack
stands on the beach,
lit only by the
shimmer of
a waxing moon.
Inside, soldiers wearing
woolen caps and wrapped in blankets gather around an oil lantern to check the
credentials of journalists crossing the river from Tajikistan. They take their time, examining
passports, excitedly asking questions and joking with the edgy foreigners.
Only a nod of approval from their commander can open the journey toward Kabul.

A set of dirt tracks, welded into hard clay by tanks and hardened by years of drought, meanders from the shack through a dusty plain. Dilapidated jeeps speed through the carved path, blinding the cars behind them with a torrent of dust as they zigzag in the direction of Kabul from the northeastern corridor. The mountain air is cold, the desert climate dry. Only the light of the moon and the weak headlights of the jeeps slice through the inky night.

There are many roads that lead to Kabul, snaking from the depths of the Afghan desert to the peaks of the Hindu Kush. But at the time we show our passports at the Afghan-Tajik border — one month after the fateful attack on New York's World Trade Center — only one originates in territory not controlled by the ruling Taliban. It is the road we will follow, in fits and starts and finally in one mad dash, to the capital, Kabul.

This road becomes more than a route of transport for us. As we follow three decades of invisible footprints thrust forward by war, it becomes a symbol for Afghanistan itself, of the brutality it has long faced and may yet endure again. Warriors and war widows, Soviet soldiers and Mujahideen rebels, invaders and defenders — all have traveled down this road before. From the dust-covered window of our jeep, and later on the front lines, we see the road and the war intertwined into a timeless and symbiotic lock, a sinewy strand of life and death that reflects the desperation and deprivation of Afghanistan today.

The war that precipitated the latest cycle of bloodletting began on Christmas Eve, 1979. The Red Army barreled down the road to Kabul in tanks, teenage soldiers at the helm. But the fighting that ensued was nothing new. Invasion, war, bribery, liberation and subjugation: they had been here for centuries. When the Soviets occupied Afghanistan and installed a puppet government the Mujahideen rose up, as their forefathers had before them, to repel the invaders. Fighting once again enveloped this desperately poor nation and with it came all the typical ingredients of Afghan warfare: brutality, greed, famine, and poverty.

War rolled over Afghan villages, destroying houses, buildings and lives. The Mujahideen fought back with ingenuity, their knowledge of the mountainous terrain canceling out the Soviets' technological superiority. When columns of Soviet tanks made their way down the narrow mountain roads, Afghan soldiers would take out the first and last tank and kill those stuck in between. Soviet soldiers never saw where the fire came from. By 1986, with no hope of victory and spooked by the Afghan ability to sow terror unseen from the mountains above, the Soviet army went home.

But the war continued. Afghan warlords fought bitterly in the power vacuum. Shells rained down on the capital, killing thousands. In 1994, the wounded country was ripe for takeover. The people, battered and broken by war, were ready to accept anyone who promised peace. A mysterious group of religious students educated in Pakistan filled the vacuum with fundamentalist zeal. Led by a young fanatic named Mullah Mohammed Omar, the Taliban took the southern city of Kandahar, the first of many victories that forced the remnant of the Afghan government to unite as the Northern Alliance and retreat.

The Taliban, with their extreme brand of Islam, began turning back the clock, attempting to bring life in Afghanistan in line with that depicted in the Koran — seventh-century Arabia at the time of Prophet Mohammed. The only place completely out of the Taliban's hard-line rule was the area controlled by Ahmad Shah Massoud and his Northern Alliance army, some ten percent of Afghanistan in the war-torn mountains of the north. At the heart of this oyster lay the pearl, the Panshjir Valley, a rebel sanctuary which Massoud managed to keep out of the hands of the Soviets and the Taliban. It was for this that he came to be known the Lion of Panshjir.

We join the Northern Alliance in Panshjir to witness the latest in a long line of victorious marches down the battered road to Kabul. The United

States is bombing Taliban-controlled territory, in response to the regime's harboring of the Al Qaeda terrorist network held responsible for the World Trade Center attack. But the little-known opposition army that welcomes us into their corner of Afghanistan is nervous and uncertain of the future. "If Massoud was still alive, we would have already liberated Kabul," a soldier's voice resonates through the colorless night as we cross the Amu Dar'ya River into Afghanistan.

Carried by an old Soviet military jeep, we steer south into a land seemingly untouched by time, scarred by war. Zigzagging up steep, rock-strewn cliffs, and flying down into lush, green valleys littered with discarded Soviet tanks, we stop only to sip over sweetened tea at guest houses, or throw our sleeping bags down on a carpet for a few hours of sleep. Dust storms rage overhead, as we pass villages whose inhabitants live in mud hovels burrowed into the rocky precipice.

Our jeep breaks down often, before roaring back to life to carry us over destroyed bridges and gushing white water. War greets us with every curve of the craggy road. Children play on the twisted bodies of artillery trucks, which were left behind to rust on dusty planes littered with land mines. Soldiers, stuffed into the beds of green Kamaz trucks, wave and shout victoriously as they pass us. Posters of Massoud are taped to the windshield of every jeep and Datsun truck.

We stop just south of the Panshjir Valley, on the Shomali Plain. The Northern Alliance, though bitter from years of being snubbed by the West, is desperate for help to win back Afghanistan. However, weeks after the bombing began, the opposition army is stalling, opting to observe rather than advance as American bombers take out vital Taliban buildings: factories, communication posts, the homes of leaders. When Kabul eventually falls from the hands of the Taliban, the justification is found deserted in Al Qaeda compounds – instructions for building bombs, anthrax leaflets and advertisements for flight schools.

Back on the Shomali Plain, the mood changes quickly after weeks of relative quiet. American bombers intensify their attack, but the rag-tag opposition army doesn't budge. "We don't have enough ammunition." "The Taliban outnumber us three to one." "We're waiting for America to bomb the front lines." Then suddenly, the rhetoric has a new twist. "We are prepared for an offensive." "As soon as you give the order, we will be ready to die."

The soldiers are ill prepared by Western army standards, but then again, this is not a Western war. Decked-out in brand new uniforms imported from China, the opposition army gathers on a dusty plane fifty miles north of Kabul for a three-day military exercise. The soldiers march out of line – some sport rubber slippers with their fatigues, others carry Kalashnikov rifles patched-up with tape. They shout "God is great!" waving posters of Ahmad Shah Massoud against a backdrop of mushroom smoke from American bombs dropped on nearby Taliban positions. After three days of relative quiet, the B-52s have resumed their systematic attack. An all out offensive, with US air support and Northern Alliance ground troops, seems imminent.

The Northern Alliance army gathers around a diagram that explains the exercise – smoking an Osama Bin Laden from his lair. The soldiers run off, firing fusillades from recoilless rifles into the hillside. Red ribbons of tracer fire fly through the sky and the boom of artillery vibrates through our stomachs. They aim at piles of white rocks, meant to represent the mastermind of terrorism, and they miss. When the dust storm picks up, the soldiers eagerly disassemble, running en masse toward home.

America is getting anxious and the holy month of Ramadan begins in a week – the Northern Alliance can't stall any longer. The security guard at our house is a soldier. "They've called us to fight," Ahmid beams as he dances around the courtyard, short-wave radio in one hand, AK-47 in the other. We set up camp at a first-aid post in the village of Bagram, not far from the airbase, where the Taliban and the Northern Alliance are sure to have a standoff. The nurses are kind to give us shelter, but they warn us that we can't stay for long. They are expecting to get busy. The next morning, we throw our mats and our backpacks into the bed of a Datsun pick-up and head for the front. When we arrive at the airbase, it is empty save for a couple of armed teenagers in fatigues. We walk up and down the road that runs parallel to the front line, amazed by the quiet and calm. Just as we consider leaving to check out another front, jeeps and military trucks drive up in a cloud of dust, and hundreds of soldiers quickly unload.

Commander Baba Jan tells us, "We are all on alert, but we haven't received any orders to attack." We follow the activity, as soldiers and tanks move into position. And then we sit. It is 11:30 in the morning, preparations for an attack are seemingly in full swing, and yet nothing is happening. Soldiers slowly drift away from the front lines and take up new positions, hanging from the windows of derelict, clay houses or lounging

in the sun by the side of the road. U.S. B-52s loop overhead, their vapor trails waving in the blue above the air base, their bombs dropping on Taliban positions. Freshly discarded apple cores litter the yards. One young soldier follows the scene with his Sony hand-cam.

"I'm happy. I'm not afraid," says Latif, 22, who like most Afghans has only one name. His fellow soldiers nod in agreement. "We are proud to be martyrs. We want to take our land back." We join Captain Habib on the roof of an abandoned house and watch him as he carefully coordinates the battle from his radio. Three tanks blast forward across the deserted airbase. From our position we can't see any soldiers or trenches – just tanks pushing through plumes of smoke. "We went past the house! We went past the house!" The field commanders have already swept past Taliban positions. They radio the Captain and ask him to move the artillery forward – they are so far ahead that they risk being hit by the Alliance's shelling.

By 3 p.m., soldiers and local villagers are returning with victory prizes. A captured Taliban truck rolls in from the front, followed by a jeep with an anti-aircraft gun. One man carries a recoilless rifle, its stock still warm from the battle, on the back of his bicycle. He says he took it off a dead Taliban soldier as he proudly pulls out the turban of the gun's former owner. "I'm going to wrap my head with it," he jokes, before wheeling his spoils home.

The Taliban quickly retreats, the battle does not last longer than an hour and just like that, the road to Kabul opens before us.

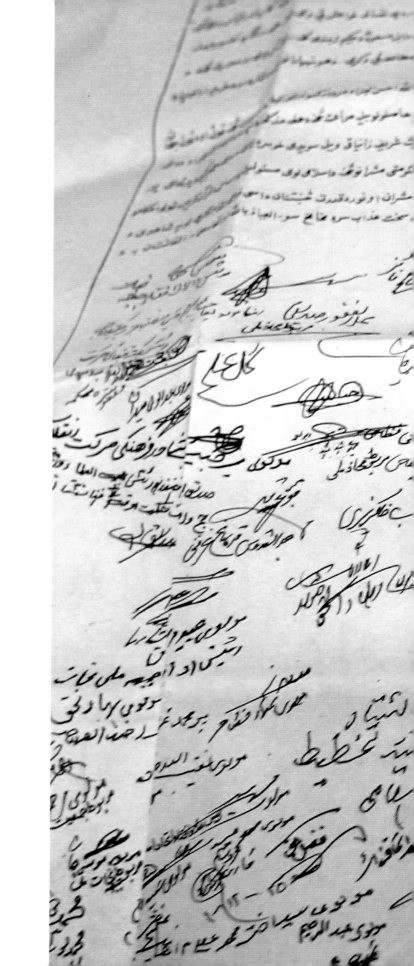

اعلان خرگنگ: افغانستان اسلامي جملہ امرونگ... والصلوة والسلام علی سید المرسلین و علی آلہ

ننگ پر تولید ود فی انشاء العزیم... نقہ کی ستی جہاد اسلامی و حکومت شیخ ترای خود شہید او
طہر جارہ از ہل ... او دی خنی باد ای علی ای استجرو دو او خپر مشا او عقلامرو کریم خویتیجہ ف شدہ لیلی سوی جہد ارنگ دالمجمورہ او اشنوزا و شرخبرہ
سولو خو پاند ی مدرسہ ماتھ المؤمنین یا مدرسہ بی جائزہ... و غیرہ مبارک نومونہ ذیکل کیر ... الحیاۃ باللہ حکم جہ دالوی تومین دہ شان دا زواج مطہر قور دی من
و ہل او تمنید او حضرت صد مسلمانانو نجو دفرض عباب قرغی بفہ مصوب استاد او پہ نظرہ مذکورہ نوای جدا او تاکیدا اغہ نبتا کوی چہ مسلمانانی بچو یہ و مکتبونو تعلیم
قرآنی آیت کریمہ ان اللہ لا یغیر ما بقوم حتی یغیروا ما بانفسہم الایہ ... دا و یرہ ست چہ موجودہ کا میاب یہ پہ نامی کامی بدلری ۱۰ عاذ نا اللہ. اوپہ مصداق الہی
تمی ثمن سلب دا عتماد بکی و شریعت دا صولو سرہ مخالفہ درہ دکری. و من التوفیق و ھو المستعان و الصلوۃ والسلام علی سید الانام و علی آلہ و اصحابہ و اتباعہ الی آخر الایام

(document contains numerous handwritten Arabic/Persian signatures across the page)

I AM GOING TO STAY AWAY FROM MINES SO I DO

MASSOUD, TWELVE YEARS OLD

We swerve off the Old Road to Kabul and onto a dirt path that leads us to the Northern Alliance command post near the village of Estergech.

N'T LOSE MY OTHER LEG

We are just
40 kilometers north of Kabul. The path
skirts the east side
of the Taliban's
horseshoe-shaped
position,
less than one kilometer away. We leave the jeep and walk over dust mounds and
prickly weeds.
A crumbling
mud wall to our right hides us from
the Taliban fighters.

A medieval, clay fortress stands in the middle of a deserted village. The command post, yet another mud hut towering over empty trenches, stands several hundred meters ahead. "You must run through quickly so the Taliban doesn't shoot you," our guide tells us as we reach an opening in the wall. We nervously lunge forward. The soldiers erupt with laughter and follow with less urgency.

After 22 years of war, this is a common reaction for Afghan fighters who can only laugh in the face of incoming fire. Heartfelt and genuine, laughter is an infectious contradiction of life in this war-ravaged land.

Despite so many years of fighting, or perhaps because of it, individual life seems to have little value in Afghanistan. The average man lives to the age of 46, a short life continually threatened by shelling, ambush and disease. The latest generation of Northern Alliance fighters is born into war and bred on defeat. Life in the north, devoid of even the most basic amenities, is grueling. The fighters often leave their families behind in Kabul when they join the opposition army. Despite the repressive Taliban regime, the quality of life in Kabul is relatively comfortable.

As the Northern Alliance prepares to launch an offensive to take Kabul, the commander of the troops north of Kabul, Bismallah Khan, appeals to his leadership in an apocalyptic overture, declaring: "As soon as you give the order, we will be ready to die." Soldiers – some grizzled veterans, others mere boys – assert their fearlessness and the belief that their fate is in God's hands. They confront war with the confidence of a man immunized against a disease. They dream of martyrdom with the conviction of a suicide bomber.

Before September 11, the Western world cares little for this country, and even less for the rebel fighters wedged into its northern corner. Ahmad Shah Massoud, the Northern Alliance leader, is idealized as a great military mastermind and romantic tales of how he routed the Soviet army more than a decade ago decorate the dinner tables of intellectuals. Meanwhile, Massoud's soldiers suffer defeat at the hands of the Taliban. Assassinated two days before the World Trade Center attacks, he leaves behind an emaciated army that continues to dream of liberating Afghanistan.

When America joins the fight against the Taliban, the Northern Alliance grows from increasing Taliban defections. But at the front in Estergech, the trenches are empty. The commander tells us it has been this way since the Americans started bombing the village nearby. We join the soldiers for tea and sugarcoated peanuts. The sun streams through the dust-covered windows and bounces off the clay walls, which are decorated with intricate drawings of birds. At every front line, we find symbols of war, engrained into daily life in Afghanistan. Soldiers hang out in empty trenches, smoking hashish to pass the time. Commanders keep yellow canaries, which chirp uninter-rupted by the whiz of artillery or boom of outgoing fire. Intricate gardens, protected by fences made of shell casings, decorate the otherwise drab courtyards of military posts. Even the Taliban cannot resist the beauty of flowers in a barren landscape. While music and kite flying is prohibited, the Taliban issues a decree demanding that citizens stop and smell the flowers.

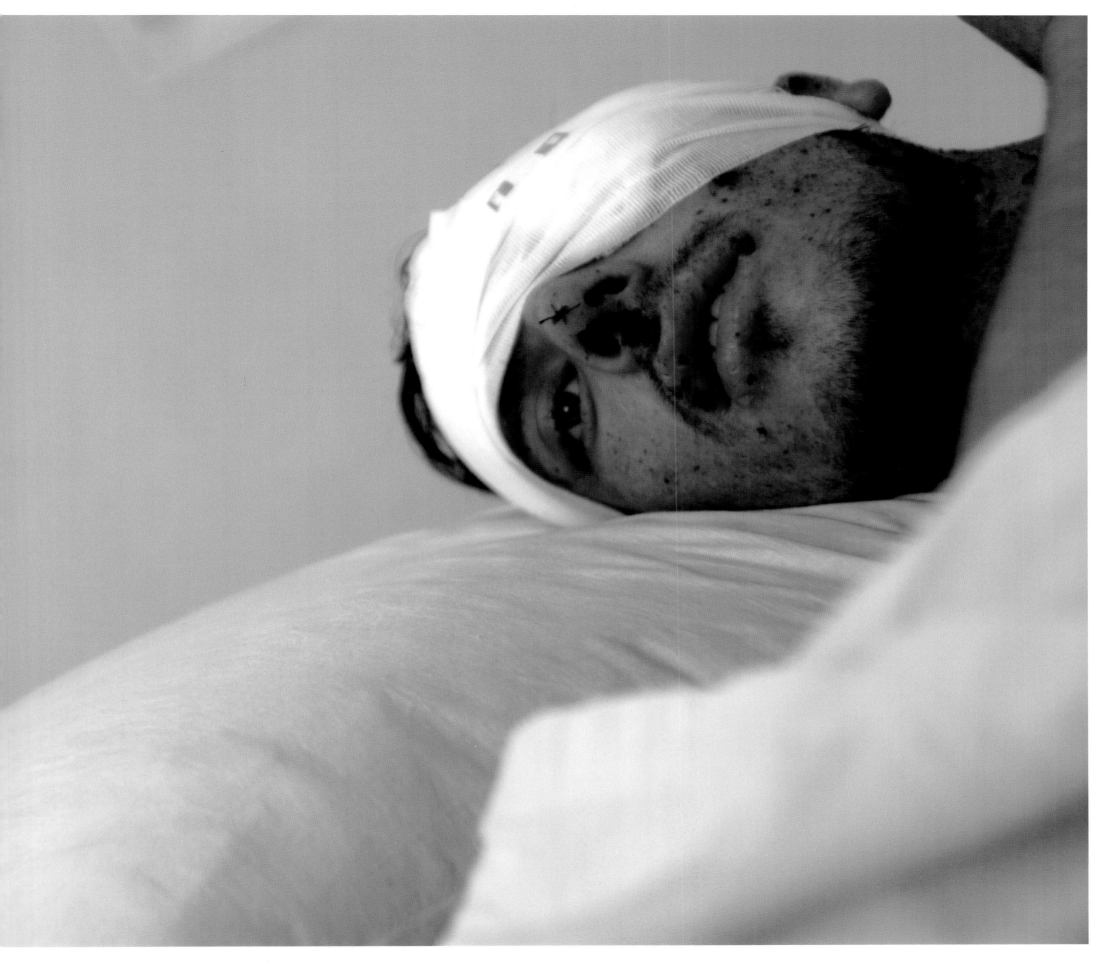

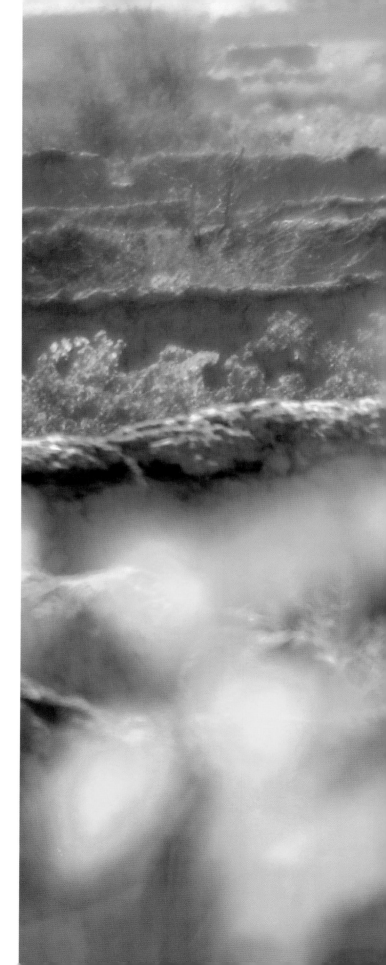

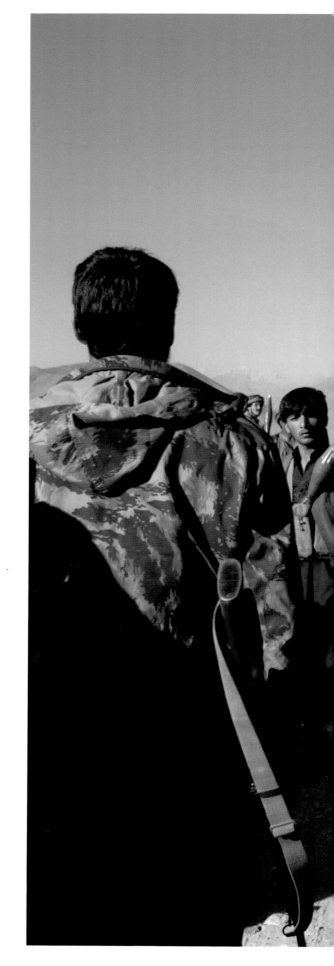

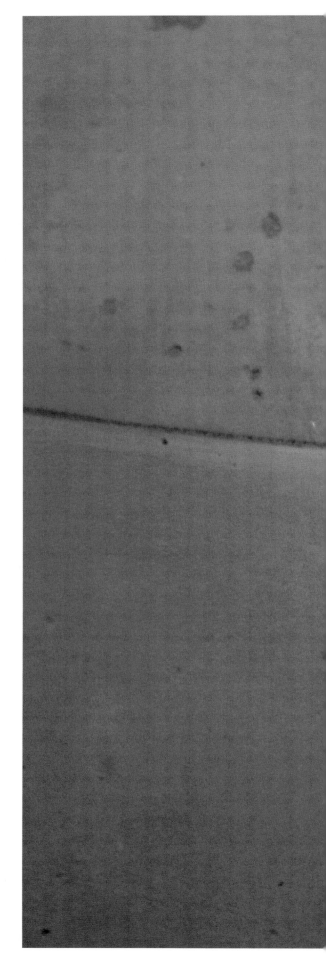

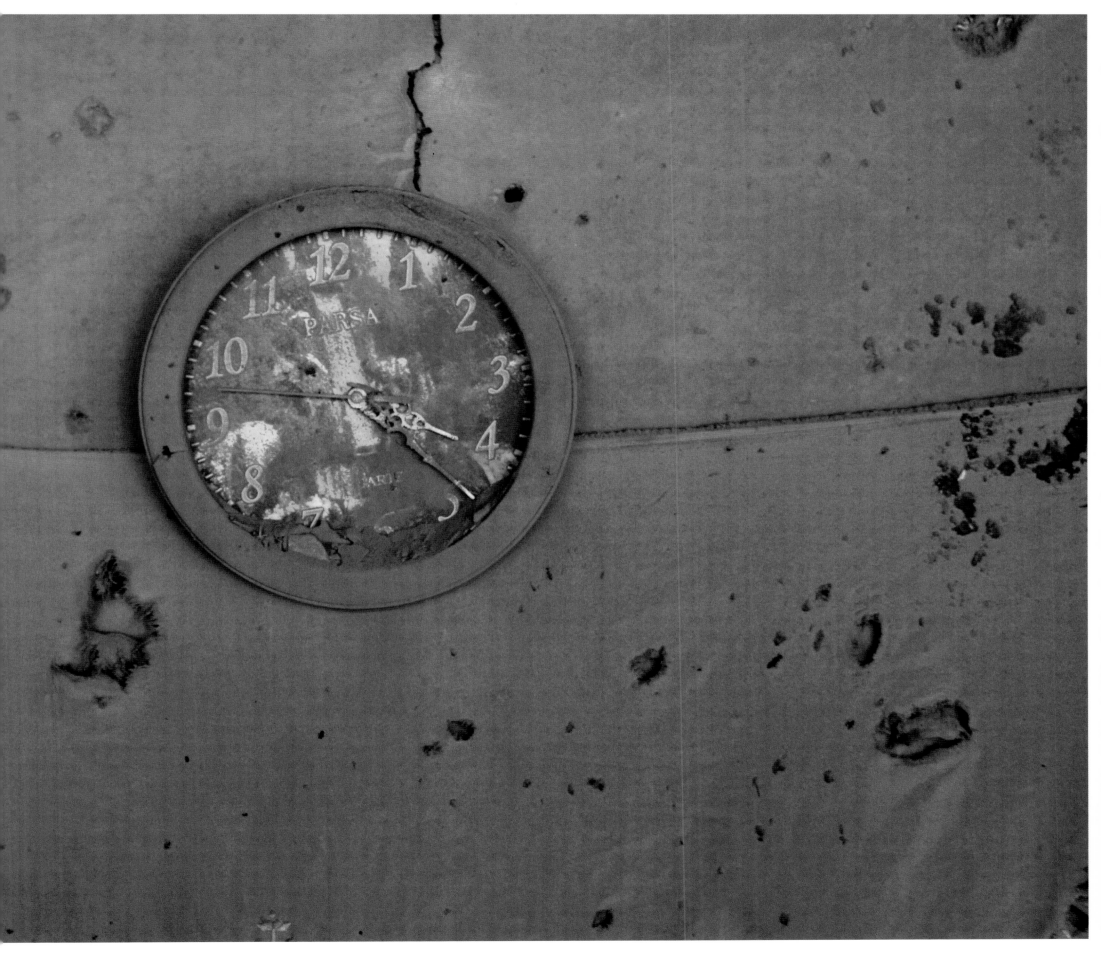

SOMETIMES WE EXCHANGE FIRE

MEXRABUDDIN, NORTHERN ALLIANCE SOLDIER

The afternoon fog is
already blanketing the
vast mountain pass
when the
Northern Alliance
soldier hops
onto the roof of his
command post

BUT IT'S NO BIG DEAL

on the peak of the Hindu
Kush and pulls out his radio. It is an ordinary day in the trenches near the
Salang Tunnel, a destroyed part of the north-south road that
has long separated the Taliban and Northern Alliance forces. Heavy snow is beginning
to roll in over the one kilometer-long no-man's land, obscuring the soldier's view.

"Star. Come in,
Star. This
is Abdullah.
Can you hear me?"
he shouts
into his walkie-talkie,
using the
code name of an
enemy Taliban
fighter just down
the road. "Hi guys!"
the broken voice
of the "Star"
answers back.
"Everything
is OK on our side.
If you don't
have anything
to report,
I'm signing off! Bye!"

Such banter across the lines is endemic to a place where brother fights brother. Later, we meet an American Special Forces soldier in northern Afghanistan who recalls how the Taliban unknowingly communicated their position to the Northern Alliance over walkie-talkies during the bombings. After a B-52 dropped a bomb on the enemy, a Taliban soldier would radio to his Northern Alliance counterpart, laughing that the bomb missed his position by 250 meters. The Northern Alliance would relay the information, the Americans would note their mistake and minutes later the bomb would fall on the right location. The American soldier tells, laughing, that it was weeks before the Taliban caught on and stopped their radio exchanges.

But the banter between enemies at the Salang Tunnel continues. When faced with two meters of snow and the boredom that comes with isolation, the ten men who live in the post at Salang find solace by conversing with the enemy. The soldiers know they are different. They cannot imagine life under the brutality and severity of the Taliban regime. They trim their beards and wear skullcaps instead of turbans. But their nightly conversations with their Taliban counterparts about subjects common to all Afghanis – family, politics, the future of the country – suggest that the only tangible difference between them is the side of the frontline they choose to sit.

There is an unmistakable permeability to the Afghan front. Information sharing and business dealings across the lines are standard operating procedures. Near the village of Dornoma, hundreds of donkeys laden with pistachios and Pepsi from Kabul trudge over the front lines. Merchants in Northern Alliance territory make weekly trips to the capital to purchase goods for their shops. They pay a small tax to the Taliban upon crossing the "border." The Taliban, in turn, relies on the Northern Alliance to print its money because no other country will do it. They buy the local currency from the opposition in dollars, and the opposition uses the dollars to buy weapons to fight the Taliban. The fluidity of the Afghan war fuels continual defections, shifting front lines and violent power vacuums. Families wake-up to find themselves suddenly living on the wrong side of the front line. This creates thousands of internal refugees, who are seen squatting in abandoned houses or living in tents on the side of the road. Soldiers fight side-by-side with men they once fought against. The enemy knocks on the door often; sometimes it is your neighbor, but likely it is your brother.

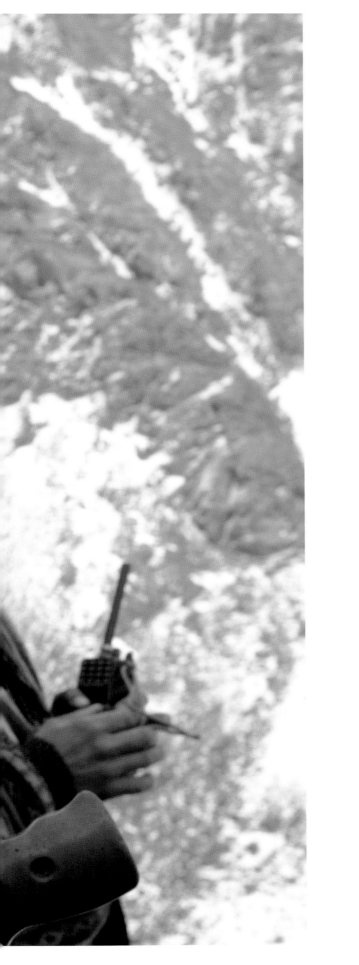

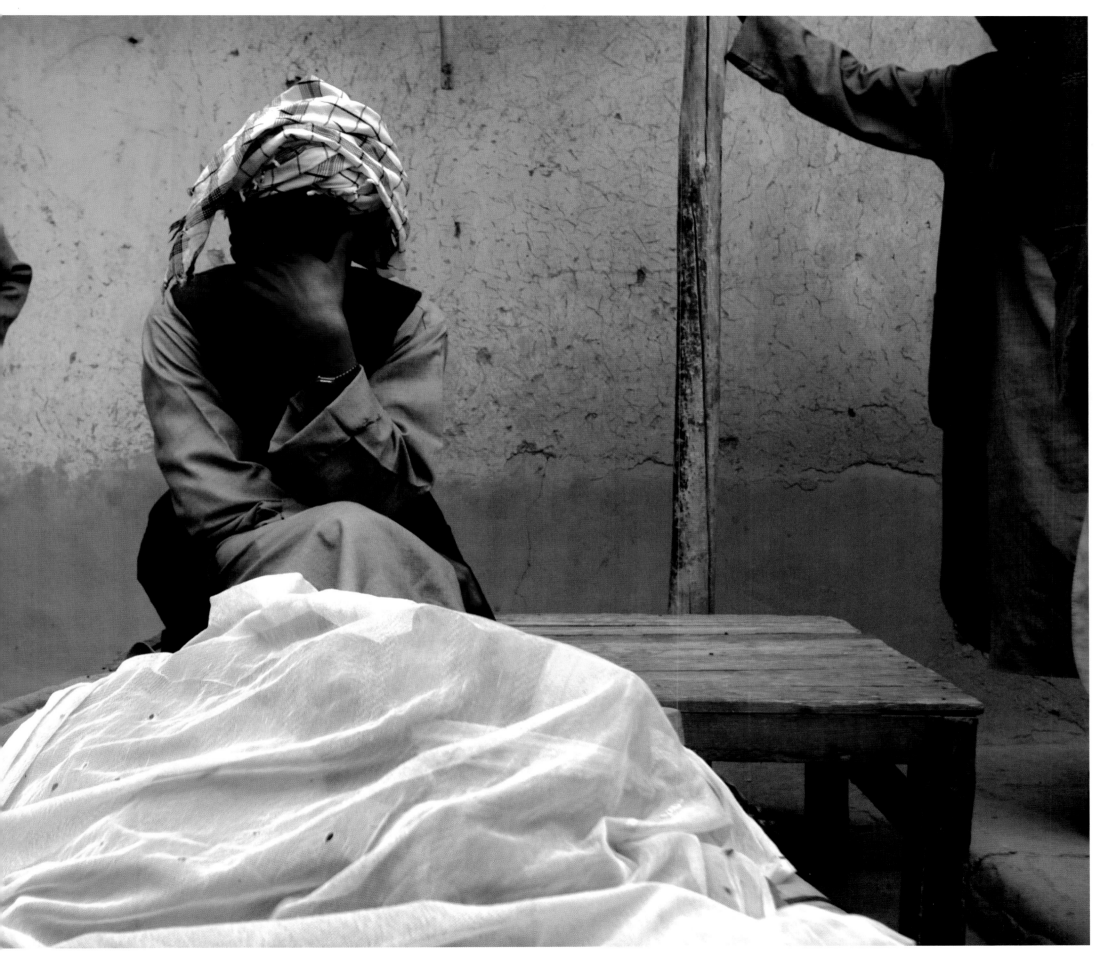

NOW I HAVE CONTROL OF MY BEARD!

ABDUL RAKHMAN, AFTER THE TALIBAN ABANDONS KABUL

It is liberation day
in Kabul,
and the road to the
capital from
northern Afghanistan
is a barren
wasteland.
Military trucks
navigate around
deep, black craters
from American
bombs,
which mark
former Taliban
positions.
Singed vineyards
stretch for
50 kilometers to the
outskirts of the
capital, peppered
with the clay
carcasses of
abandoned huts.
Fruit orchards
once stood
along the road, but
they were
chopped down
by the Taliban
to get a better
view of the enemy.
Only the tree stumps
remain, filling
the dry fields like
headstones
in a graveyard.

Two Northern Alliance soldiers walk slowly toward Kabul, careful not to stray off the cracked tarmac into mine-packed fields. They hold each other's hand, with Kalashnikovs casually slung over traditional Afghan outfits of long shirt and baggy pants. Yesterday, their stroll through no-man's land was inconceivable. Today, the road to Kabul stretches before them, promising salvation like it has so many times before.

The fun begins just hours after the Taliban regime flees Kabul. With no government in place, and lackadaisical security forces in charge of keeping the peace, the citizens of Kabul are quick to take advantage of the freedom that comes with liberation. They shout "Death to Pakistan! Death to Mullah Omar, who is a donkey!" and spit on the mutilated bodies of Arabs and Pakistanis, which were thrown into the gutters of a park after a bloody shoot-out. The foreign fighters, unaware that the Taliban had abandoned them,

had climbed onto the yellowing treetops armed with Kalashnikov rifles and fired at locals from above before turning into martyrs of a failed regime. Their lifeless mouths are stuffed with cigarettes and money, meant to mark them as corrupt.

A few hundred yards away, some men decide to take their revenge on the Taliban by looting the compound once occupied by the Taliban's religious police, The Ministry for the Prevention of Vice and Promotion of Virtue. They ransack the compound, careful in their fury to bypass the stacks of holy Korans, and leave behind a trail of scattered religious edicts and whips, which were once used to punish disobedient citizens for not trimming their beards or being late for prayer time.

Other forms of celebration are taking place across town. Kites fly high in the sky, a decadence forbidden by the Taliban. Music blasts from bazaar stalls and taxi radios for the first time in five years. A Northern Alliance flag drapes the gates to the foreign ministry. Years of ascetic living leave an imprint on the people of Kabul and there is no burqa-burning revolution in the aftermath. Women wander out from behind painted windows, their faces hidden underneath blue, floor-length robes. Their small token of freedom is noted in the absence of a male relative escort, as they glide like ghosts down the dusty streets.

Men crowd into barbershops to trim their beards, but few dare to take a razor to their skin. "Before the Taliban, I didn't have a beard," says Maidanshare, after the barber chops half an inch of his thick, black beard. He is ashamed to go any further. "I won't shave it off completely. A man with no beard is not attractive," he says.

By afternoon, it is back to business as usual. Merchants in the bazaars re-open their stalls. Citizens no longer cheer at the increasing number of soldiers pouring into the capital. The Northern Alliance faces little resistance and the big battle for Kabul never takes place.

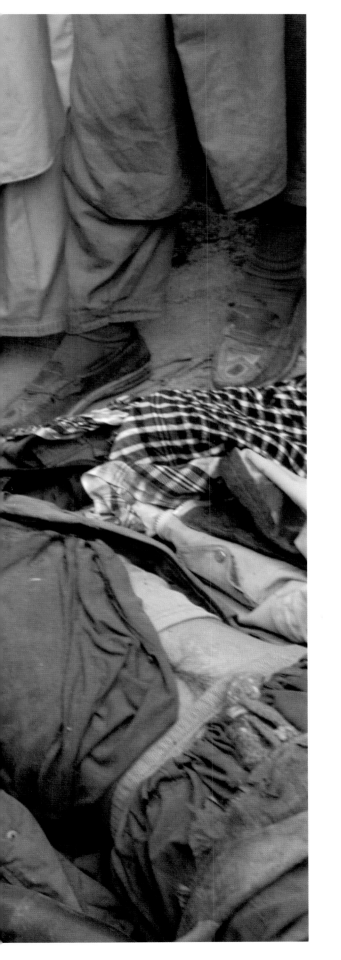

LEARN HOW TO USE THESE THINGS*

A TNT DIAGRAM FOUND IN A FORMER AL QAEDA HOUSE, KABUL

In the days after
the Northern Alliance
takes Kabul,
the locations of former
Taliban bases, as
well as the bases of
Al Qaeda, gradually
become known to
journalists. What we
find inside the
walls of these abandoned
houses and buildings
is more telling of
the war than anything
we see on the front
lines or gather
from the rehearsed
diatribes of
Northern Alliance
commanders.
Here, scattered on the
floors of makeshift
classrooms and family
residences, we
discover the real reason
America joined
the fight in Afghanistan.

One of the houses is located in an upscale neighborhood, the former diplomatic district in Kabul. It is a quaint, two-story house filled with sunlight. Instead of furniture, scraps of paper covered with doodles and diagrams lie discarded on a floor strewn with trash. English and Arabic are scrawled in blue across what were once pages in a date book. A closer look reveals that these papers are in fact a guide for making crude explosives in a bathtub. There are more papers like them, a potpourri of hundreds of leaflets littering the floors of deserted, empty rooms. Internet printouts, pages torn from chemistry textbooks, lists of names – an ominous, terrible science fair project gone wrong.

We find a page torn out of a flight magazine advertising flight schools in Florida. In another room, a smaller piece of paper lists the registration number for a Microsoft Flight Simulator, a computer program that commercial pilots use when they want to practice

landing a jumbo jet. There is a list of instructions in Arabic entitled "Before and After Precautions For Using Chemical, Biological and Nuclear Warfare." There are requisition forms addressed to "Al Qaeda Ammunition Warehouse," with the names filled in and orders for rifles and grenades. Some of the documents are partially burned.

In another building in Kabul, we find French anti-tank rockets, still in their casings and stashed behind a heavy mortar and a slew of helmets. The walls of this house are more decorous than the previous Al Qaeda residence. One wall boasts a hand-painted insignia baring two Kalashnikov rifles, crisscrossed below a Koran and the catchy slogan "Jihad is our way." Another wall is decorated with a colorful map entitled "Occupation of the Holy Lands of Islam by the Crusaders." It depicts U.S. and British military bases in the Middle East.

The empty rooms of this apartment building appear to be classrooms in a rudimentary training camp, with smaller rooms used as student and family residences. Notebooks and letters illustrate how eager, young recruits spent their days learning the teachings of the Koran, the English alphabet and how to drop balloons full of anthrax on infidels. Outside, across the shabby courtyard, there is a smaller building with apartments to house the students of this learning center. It, too, is empty, save for the land mines thrown casually across the cold, clay floor.

Journalists find several such buildings in Kabul; surely, dozens more remain undiscovered. The houses share eerily similar characteristics: weapons, plans for attack, piles of documents with references to ties in Somalia, Chechnya, Libya, Egypt, Uzbekistan, Tajikistan, Sudan, Canada and the United States. Lists of names, scores of passports and forged visas. Correspondence with Osama bin Laden, jihad proclamations, books on how to wage nuclear warfare. If authentic, it is evidence that provides insight into Al Qaeda's plotting and training in Afghanistan, as well as the breadth of Osama bin Laden's influence.

By the second week, the locals begin to hawk the materials for money. Reporters can purchase videotapes, computers and floppies, recovered from undisclosed locations by enterprising Afghans. The houses are loosely guarded, sometimes not at all. Everyone is guilty of looting and no one knows if the scraps of paper, the stockpiles of weapons, the maps, the mines are really left behind by Al Qaeda or planted in those first days after the Taliban flees. A question looms oppressively over our minds – if this is what is left, then what did they purge? More importantly, what did they take with them?

*CHRISTIAN SCIENCE MONITOR . SCOTT PETERSON 11.19.2001

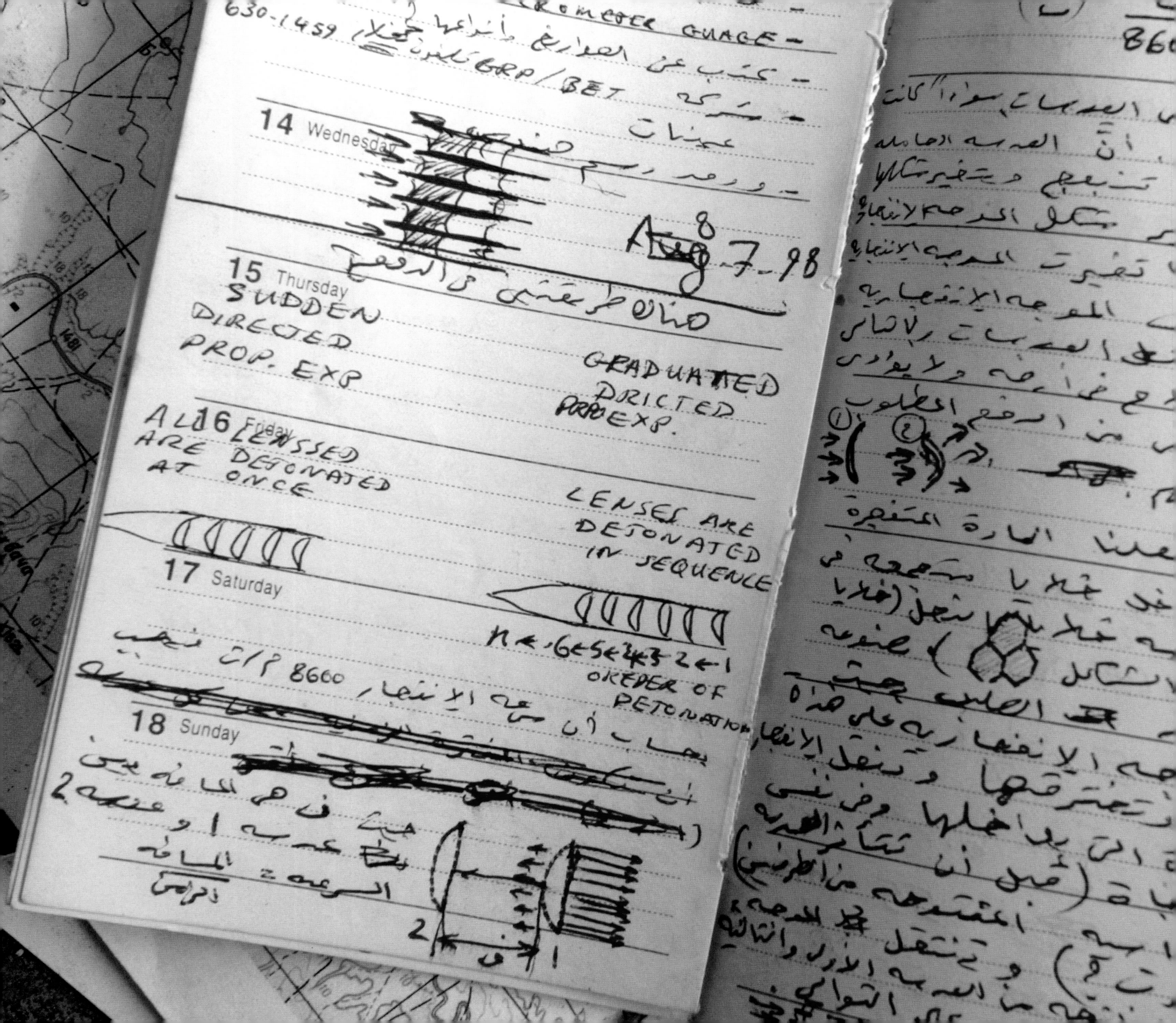

14 Wednesday

Aug 7-98

15 Thursday
SUDDEN
DIRECTED
PROP. EXP

GRADUATED
DRICTED
PROP EXP.

16 Friday
ALL LENSSED
ARE DETONATED
AT ONCE

LENSES ARE
DETONATED
IN SEQUENCE

17 Saturday

N ← 6 ← 5 ← 4 ← 3 ← 2 ← 1
ORDER OF
PETONATION

C/P 8600

18 Sunday

2   1

Tuesday 20

Wednesday 21

Thursday 22

Friday 23

Saturday 24

Sunday 25

GOD, THE NAME OF OUR COUNTRY IS DEATH. WE

MASURI, DOCTOR

It is easy to ignore
a woman in Afghanistan,
easier still to forget
she exists.
Veiled by polyester from
head to toe, she is
neither seen nor heard
in the crowded streets.

Against the desert backdrop of muted brown and yellow, the colorful contrast of blue, green and mustard-colored burqas is a sight of spectacular beauty. But it serves, too, as a painful reminder that 22 years of war has thrust women into the darkest corners of Afghan society. Women in Kabul once attended university, practiced medicine and worked as government bureaucrats. Gradually, and systematically, they were reduced to banshees who must hide from the eyes of strangers, cower in the presence of men and live out the will of their fathers and husbands. Their day-to-day struggles can take on heart

HAVE LOST OUR HAVEN TO CRUELTY

There are rare exceptions,
as when a widow
descends on strangers,
stretching out dry,
scarred hands while
a muted voice
drifts through the mesh
pleading for alms.
But even the boldest of
widows cannot convey the
deep creases that pain
has carved on her face.
They usually return
empty-handed
to float in the shadows.

breakingly comical undertones. Two women chat like co-conspirators, as their hands clutch the burqa at the neck so they can see each other better through the mesh. A man rides by on a bicycle, his wife sitting sidesaddle behind him in a burqa, her red pumps dangling beneath her. The blue outline of women stuffed into the back of a station wagon, bobbing up and down as their male relatives stretch out in the seats. A woman shopping, the only sign of her vanity are painted toes in platform, patent-leather sandals peeking out from underneath a burqa.

Every time I meet an Afghan woman for the first time, always in the safe confines of her husband's walls, I am taken aback by the emotion and affection that is so easily hidden by the burqa. The women typically greet me with an embrace. They plant six kisses on alternating cheeks, making the last one extra strong for emphasis. They always ask me if I am married and giggle as they tell me they love me. Earrings dangle from uncovered ears, while elaborate hairstyles and make-up accentuate beautiful, dark faces. The women show me their photo albums, leafing through black and white photos of their mothers in mini-skirts and newer, color photographs of engagement parties, where the groom is absent and the bride resembles a sexy "Bollywood" movie star from India. Once the Taliban flees, the real Bollywood starlets can be seen everywhere in Kabul, striking provocative poses on posters, trading cards and television sets in the bazaar. With no Taliban to whip them for impropriety, men spend their afternoon leering at the beauties.

But it is not yet time for the women of Kabul to lift the veil. A woman named Rida burns her burqa when the Taliban flees, but when she goes to the bazaar, a mob of men surround her and jeer at her open face. Though she is one of the first women to return to work in Kabul, reading the news on radio and television, Rida does not leave her house again, except to get into a taxi that whisks her to and from work. Rida's struggle is both a symbol of progress and a reminder that the burqa is at once oppressive and protective. One by one, burqas are left hanging on hooks as women brave the streets, with only a headscarf to cover them. For the women of Kabul, change is slow but quietly persistent.

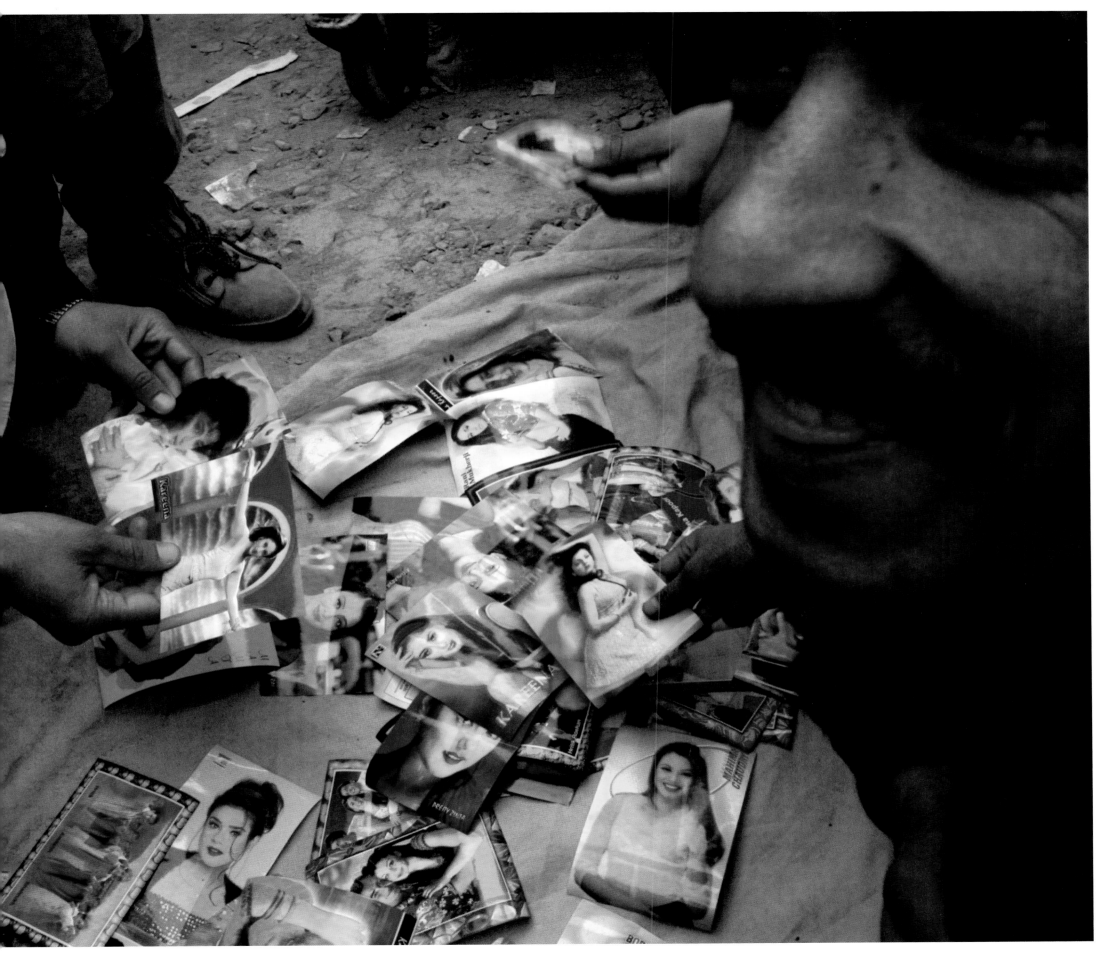

CONCLUSION

It is difficult to pin down exactly when and where we began our journey on the road to Kabul. The obvious answer is the night we climbed into that rundown jeep on the riverbank and headed south through the Afghan outback. But really, our journey began much earlier, in the days following September 11, when the name Osama bin Laden flashed across every television screen in America, when it was difficult to imagine anyother country capable of harboring this terrorist and his intricate network, when George W. Bush declared he wanted bin Laden, dead or alive.

We followed our instincts and scrambled to make our way to one of the most remote and underdeveloped countries in the world. In Afghanistan, we discovered a world of mystery and contradictory beauty, a culture so closed to the outside world that instead of delving into its malleable heart, our efforts merely chipped away at its hard, outer shell.

We also discovered what appeared too good to be true. How quickly it had all come together: the war, the bombings, the flight school advertisements on a dirty floor in Kabul. America had cornered the bad guys, the terrorists, but it was impossible to imagine peace in a country where allies turned to enemies overnight, where warlords made government bedfellows, where corruption seeped into every crack of society. War in Afghanistan had long taken on a life of its own, and it jeered into the sun burnt faces of American soldiers: "I was here before you and I will stay long after you're gone."

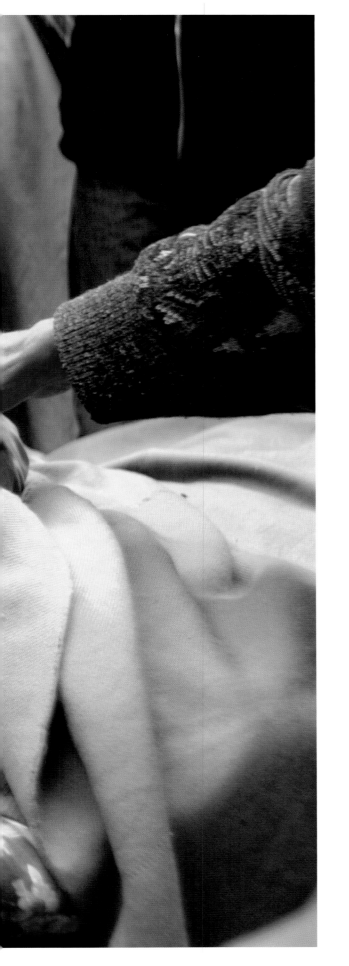

CAPTIONS

For English Language Edition . Art Direction and Design: Giorgio Baravalle . de.MO
Photo Editor: Alison Morley **Text Editor:** Robert Friedman

First published in Italy: Sulla Strada per Kabul © 2002 Federico Motta Editore S.p.A., Milano.   Printed and bound in Italy by Arti Grafiche Motta, Milano.
Published in the United States by de.MO 123 Nine Partners Lane Millbrook New York 12545. **www.de-mo.org**

Library of Congress Control Number: 2002103576   ISBN 0-9705768-5-4   Distributed by F&W Publications Inc., Cincinnati, Ohio.

This book would have not been possible without the support of Michele McNally and Scott Thode of Fortune Magazine. A grateful thank you to Robert Friedman
of Fortune for shepherding this project from start to finish. Thanks to Didier Rapaud of Paris Match and Andreas Trampe of Stern for their valuable support.
I want to thank Alison Morley for her tireless dedication and the creative editing, which brought the vision of this book to light.
The support of Ashley Woods of VII, Michele Neri and Grazia Neri brought the work from Afghanistan to the reality of a book. I would especially like to express my
gratitude, appreciation and amazement for Giorgio and Elizabeth Baravalle for their tireless dedication and belief in this book. The work of Cari Modine and Kristin
Bingman of de.MO have helped bring this vision to an appreciative audience.
Many thanks to Shazi Hussain and Art Murphy of DigiZone for their continued support and fantastic work. With gratitude to Mark Dennis and Irina Ozernoy who gave
their time and creativity to the project.
In the field I thank my colleagues and Afghan friends, Peter Blakely, Christian Caryl, Pierre Celerier, Stanley Greene, Tyler Hicks, John Kifner, Gary Knight, Marco
di Lauro, James Nachtwey, Matt McAllester, Remy Ourdan, Scott Peterson, David Rhode, Elizabeth Rubin, Moises Saman, John Stanemeyer, Stefan Smith, Ferodoon,
Masood, Nasir, Vladimir Volkov and Wahid who made the difficult journey a great adventure.
With deep gratitude to Ilana Ozernoy for her words and wisdom, which guided us on this journey and helped shape this book.
Thanks to my family for keeping me in their hearts throughout my travels. **www.VIIphoto.com**

RON HAVIV

Throughout his career as a
photojournalist Ron Haviv
has confronted risk in order to
bring our attention
to our less fortunate neighbors.
He has covered conflict in
Latin America and the Caribbean,
crisis in Africa, the Gulf War,
fighting in Russia, anarchy and
conflict in the Balkans and Afghanistan.
Ron is represented by the
VII agency and is a
contract photographer for
Newsweek. His work is
widely published by magazines
throughout the world including Time,
Esquire, German Geo,
Stern, Paris Match and the
New York Times Magazine.
His photographs have
earned him several World Press,
Picture of the Year and
Overseas Press Club awards
and the Leica Medal of Excellence.
His work has been
exhibited in major galleries and at
the United Nations,
The Newseum and
The Council on Foreign Relations.
He has contributed to
several books,
and regularly lectures
at universities and seminars.
Blood and Honey: A Balkan War Journal,
his first book is the result
of ten years of Haviv's work
in the Balkans.

ILANA OZERNOY

Ilana Ozernoy is a freelance writer
who contributed to
U.S. News and World Report,
The San Francisco Chronicle and
The Boston Globe.
She traveled the long road to Kabul
with the Northern Alliance
to write the essays for this book.